This

COLORING BOOK

BELONGS TO

____

____

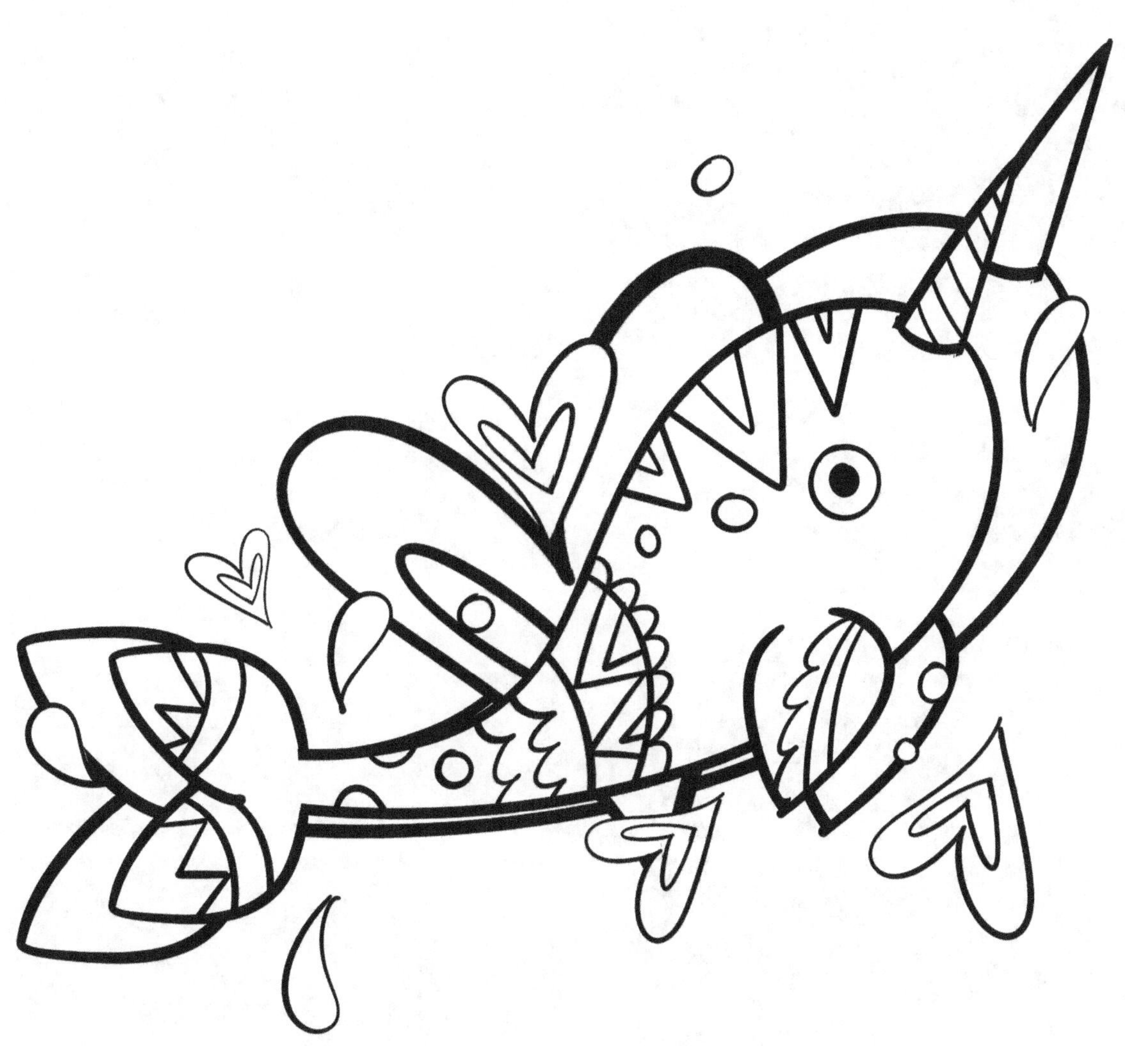

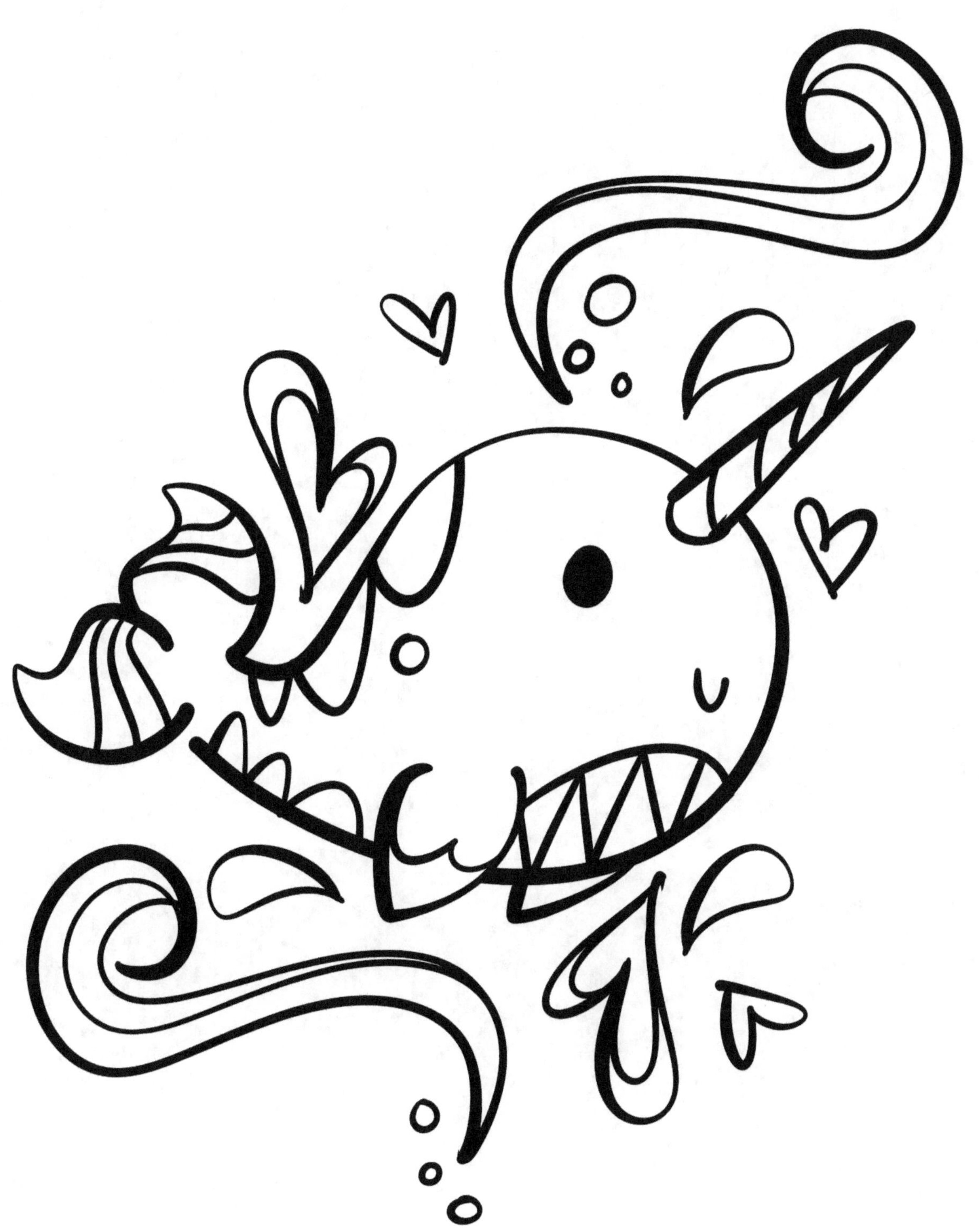

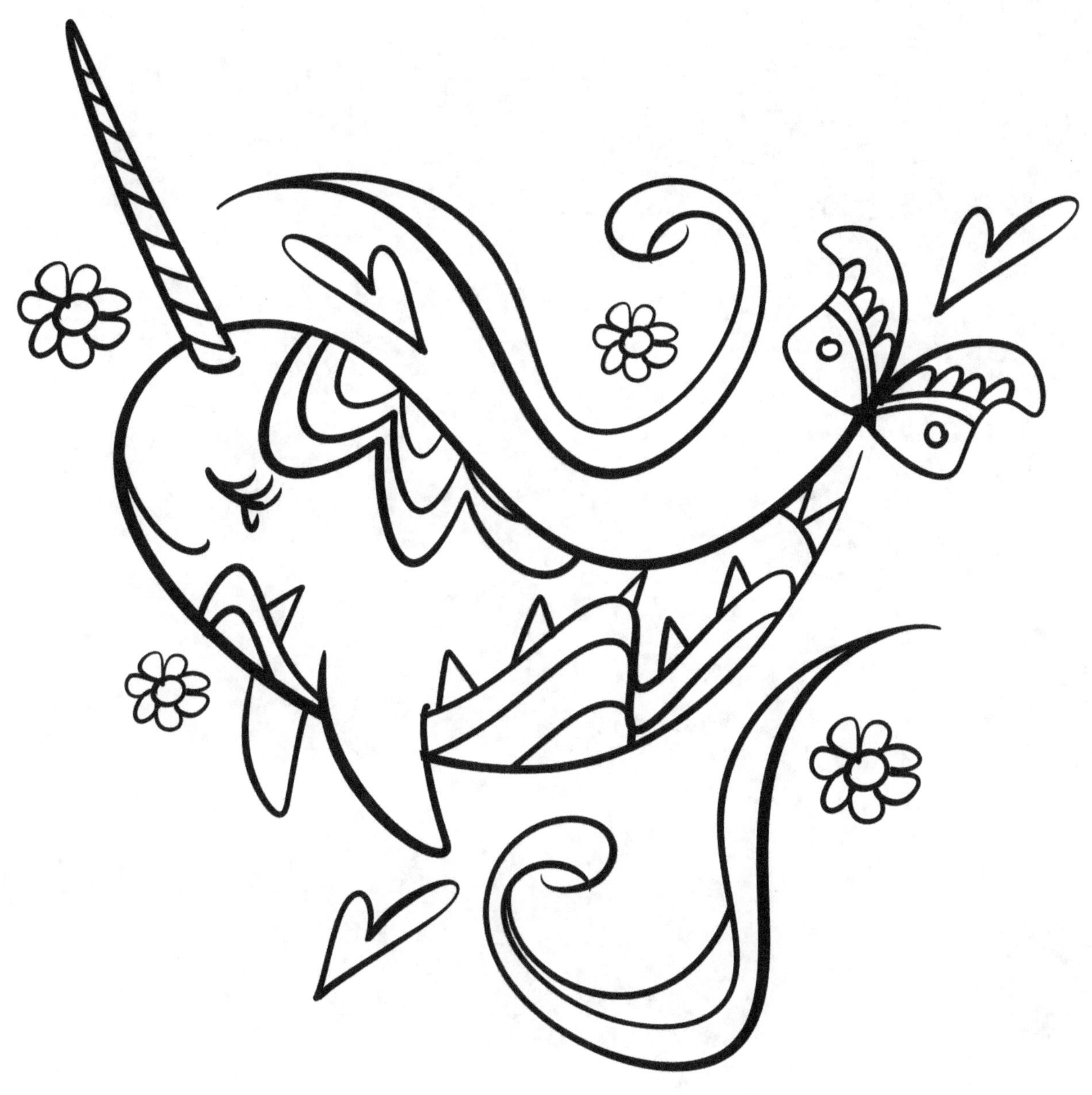

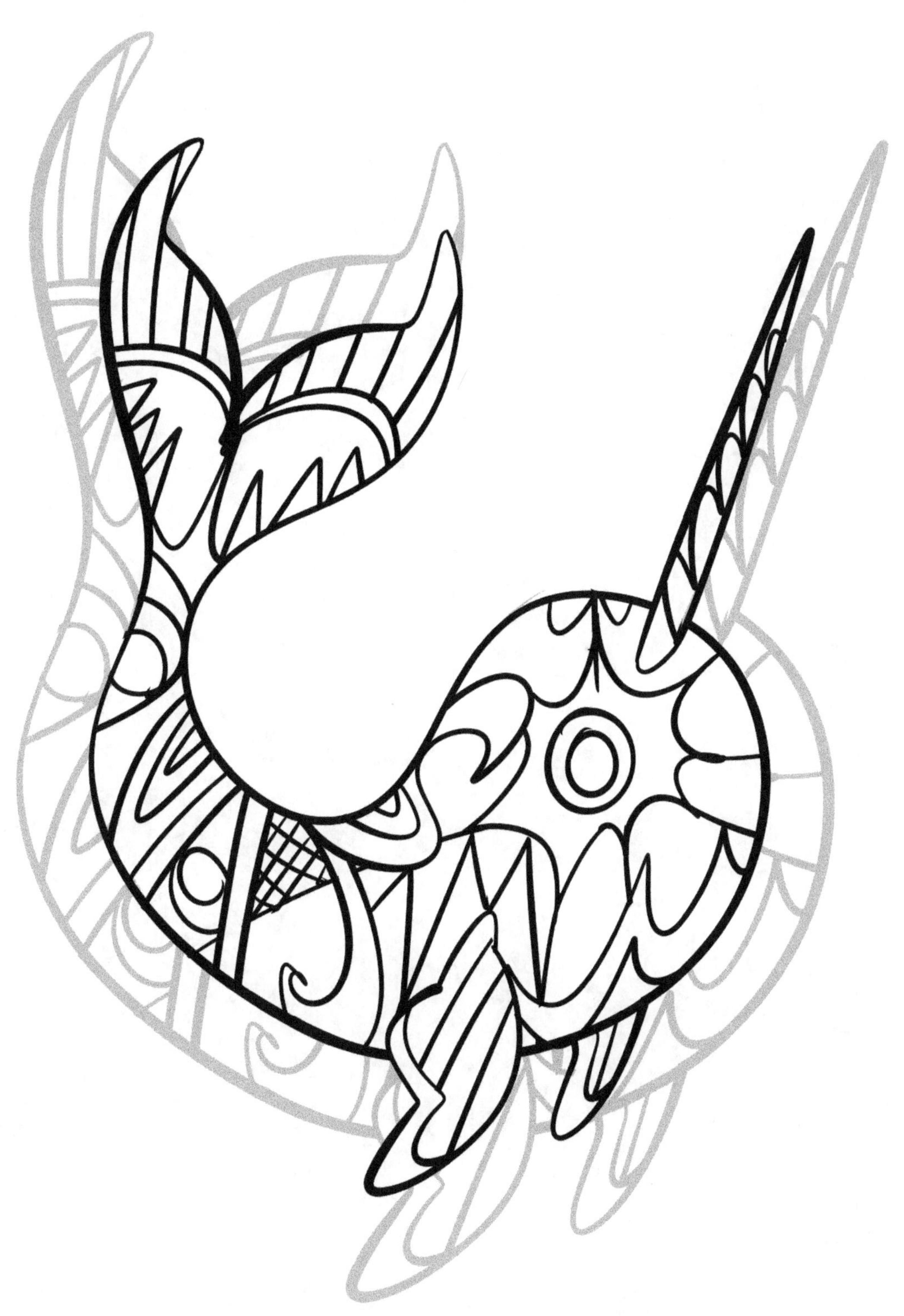

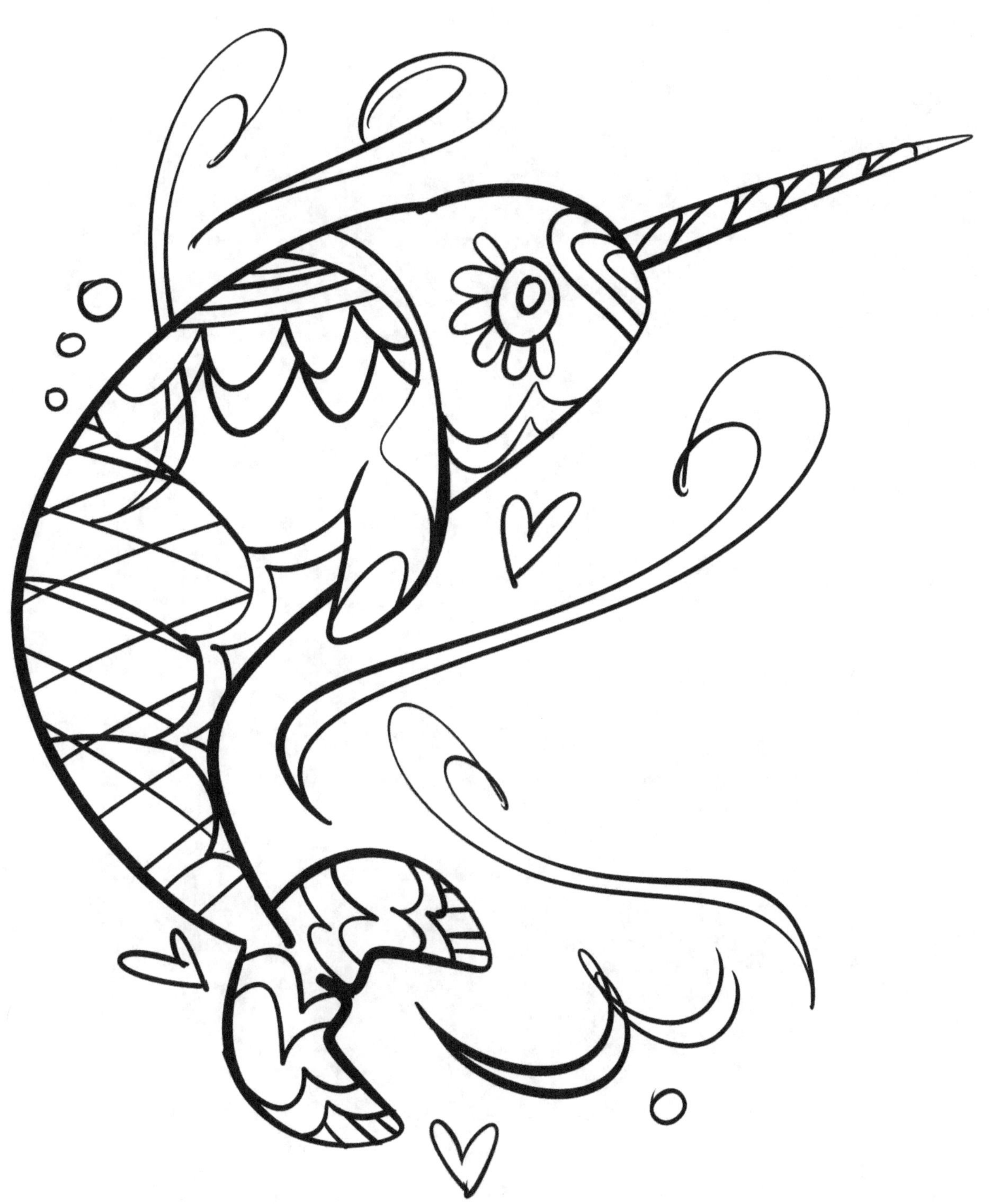

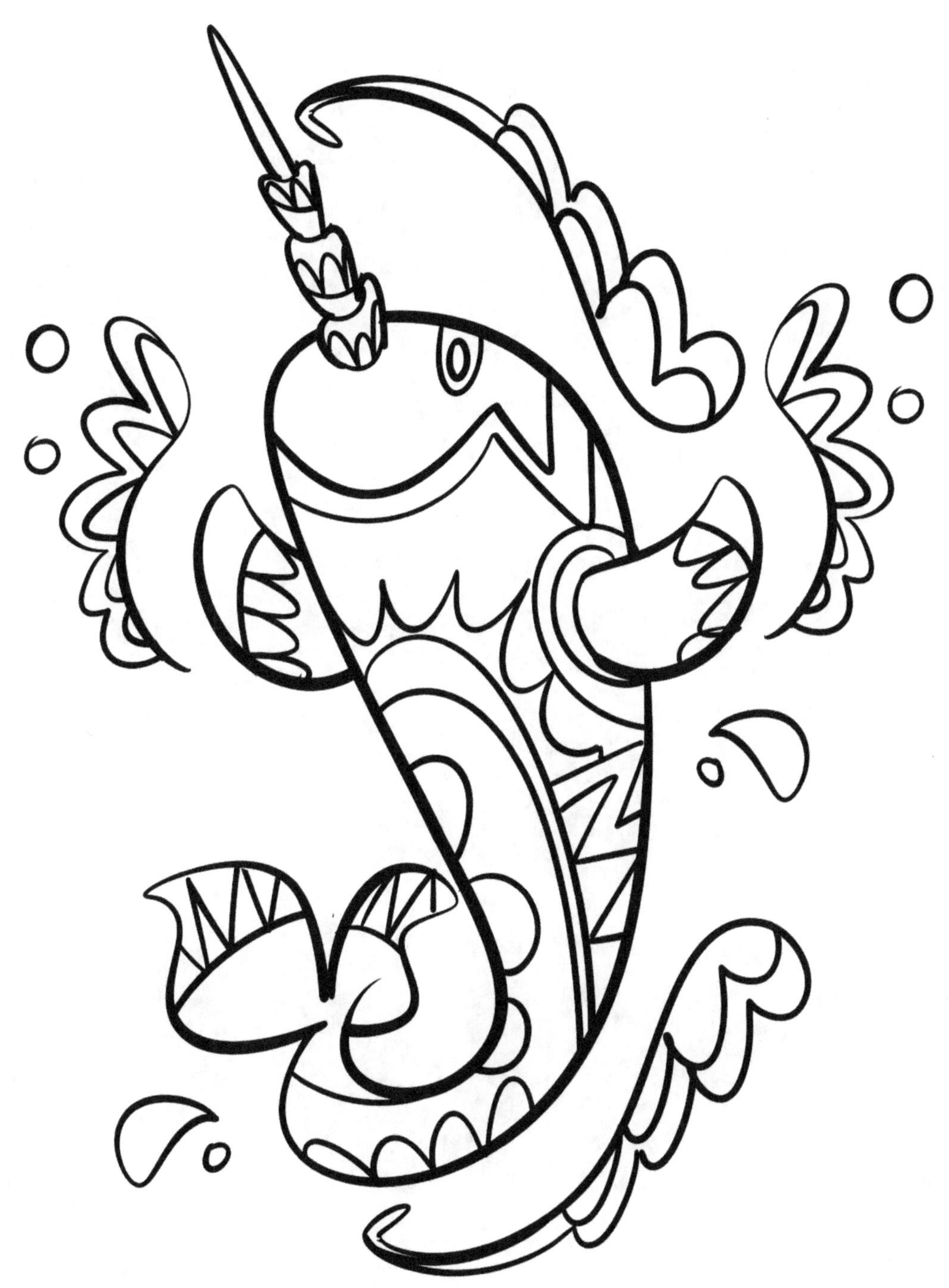

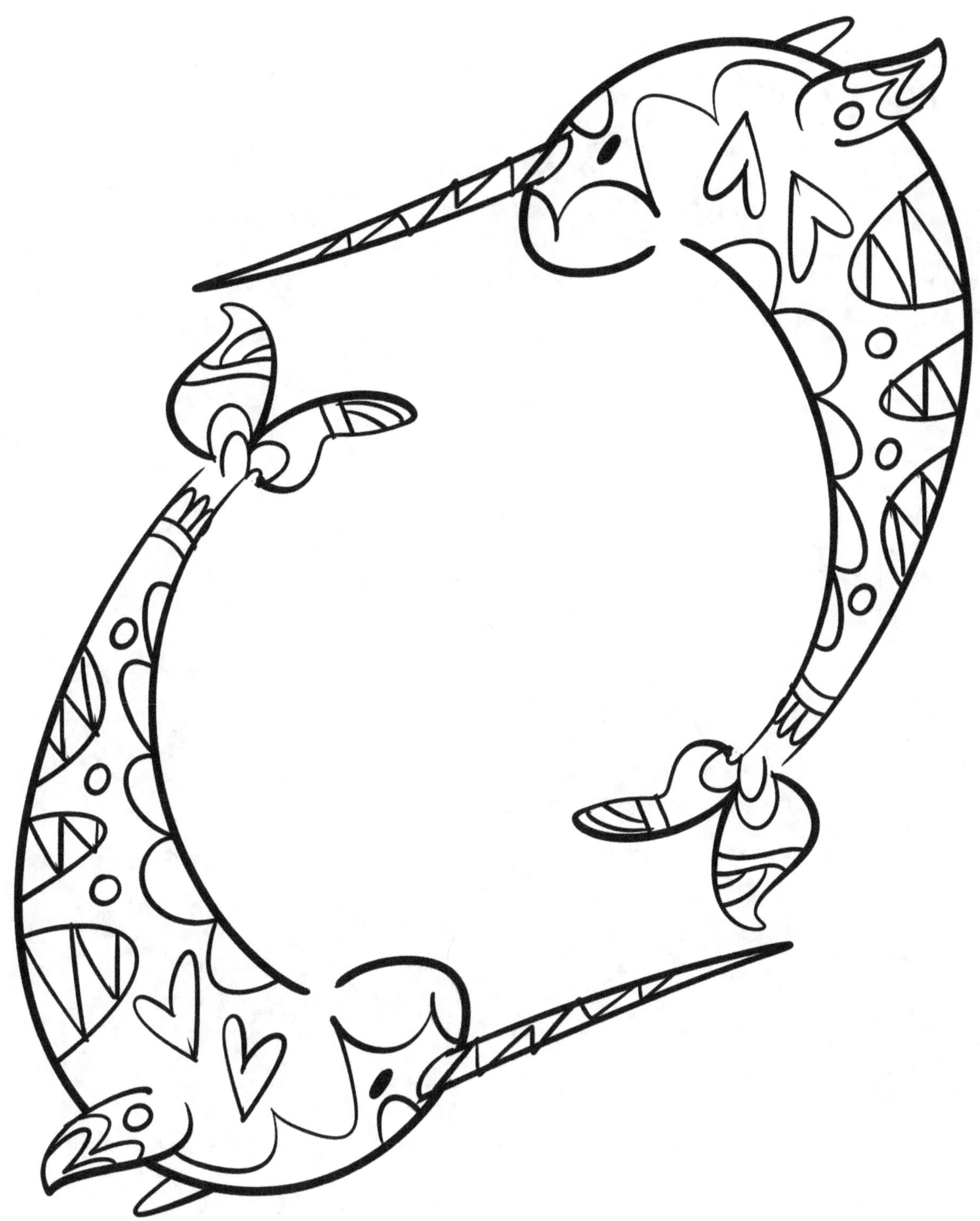

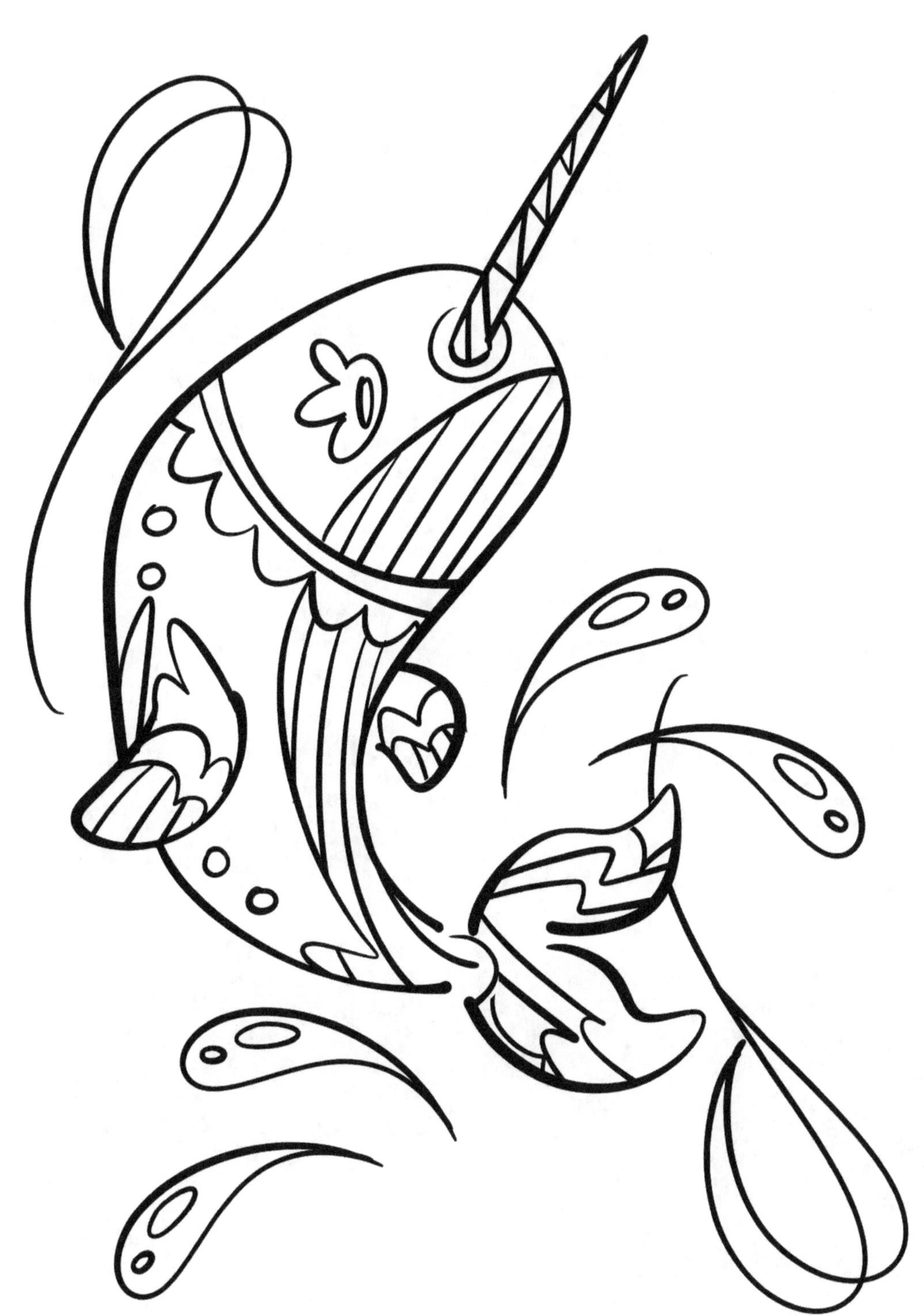

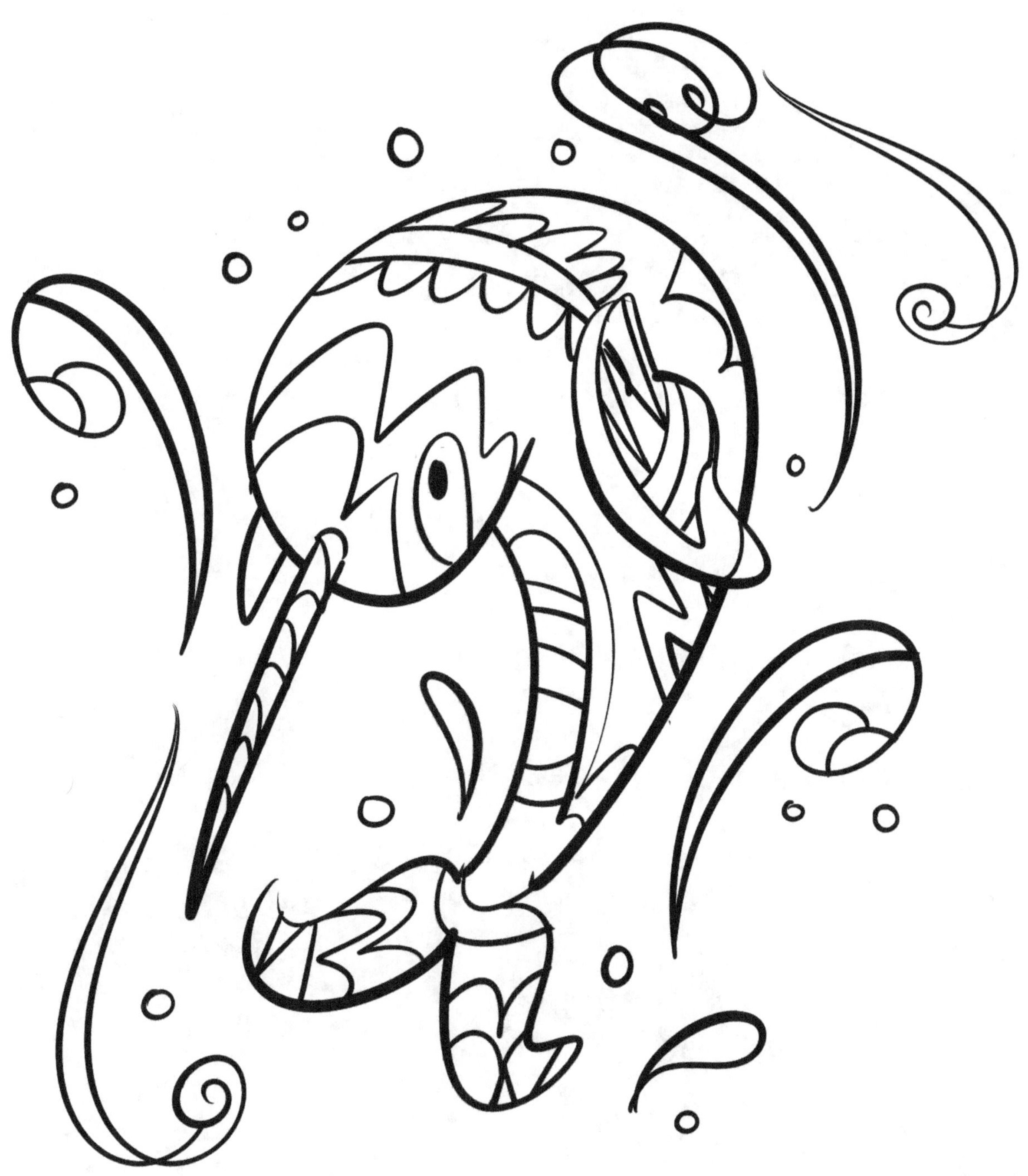

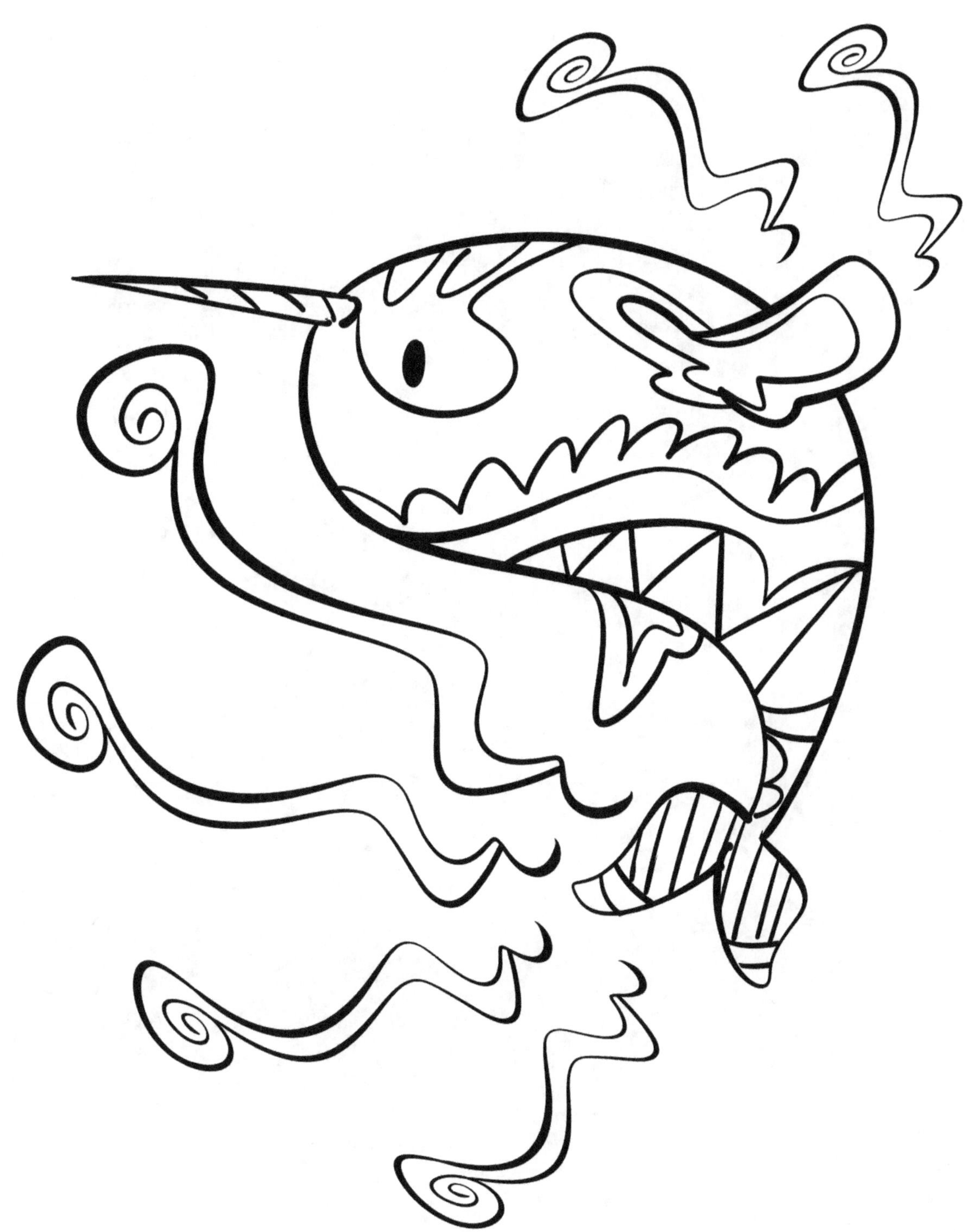

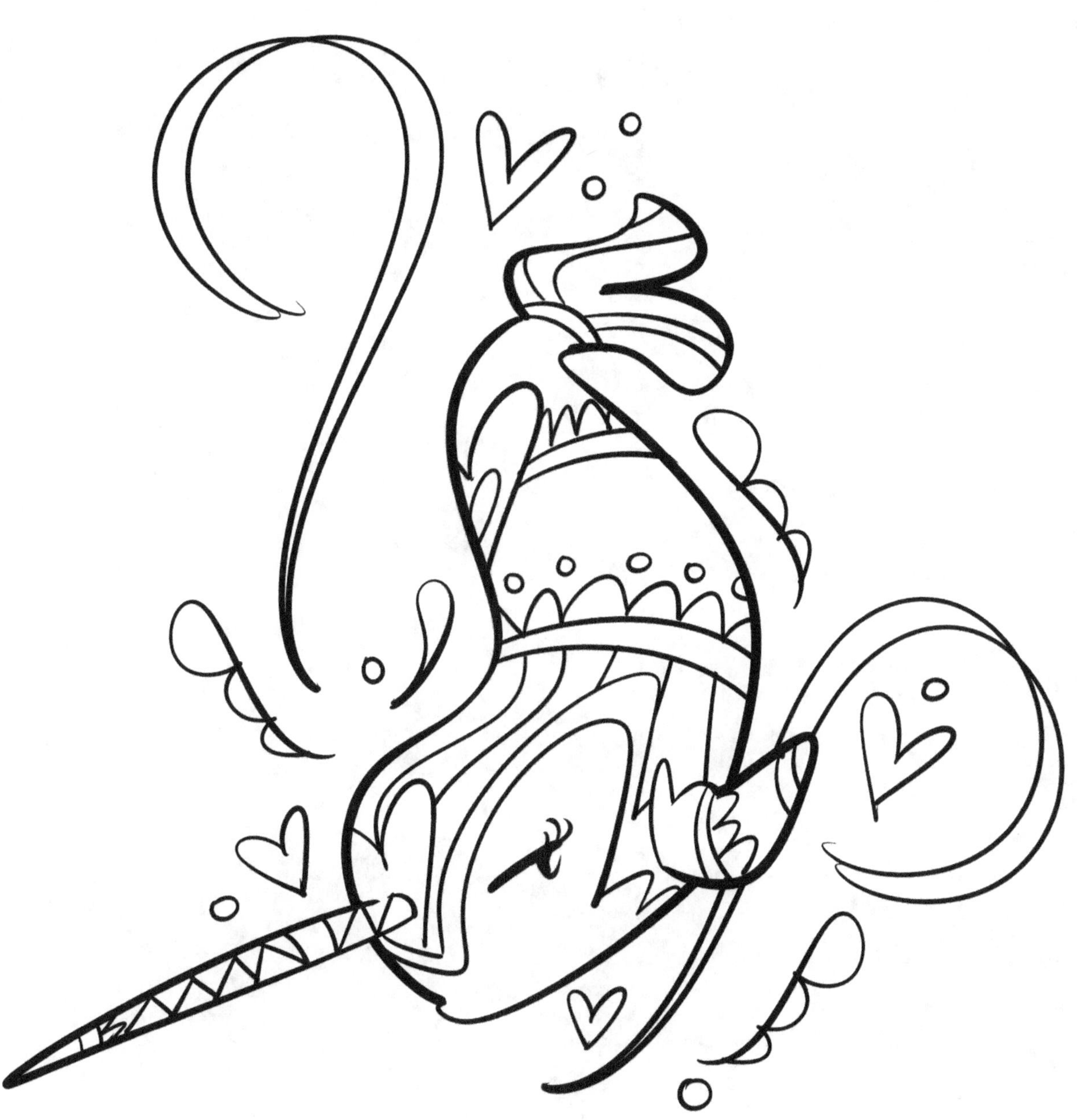

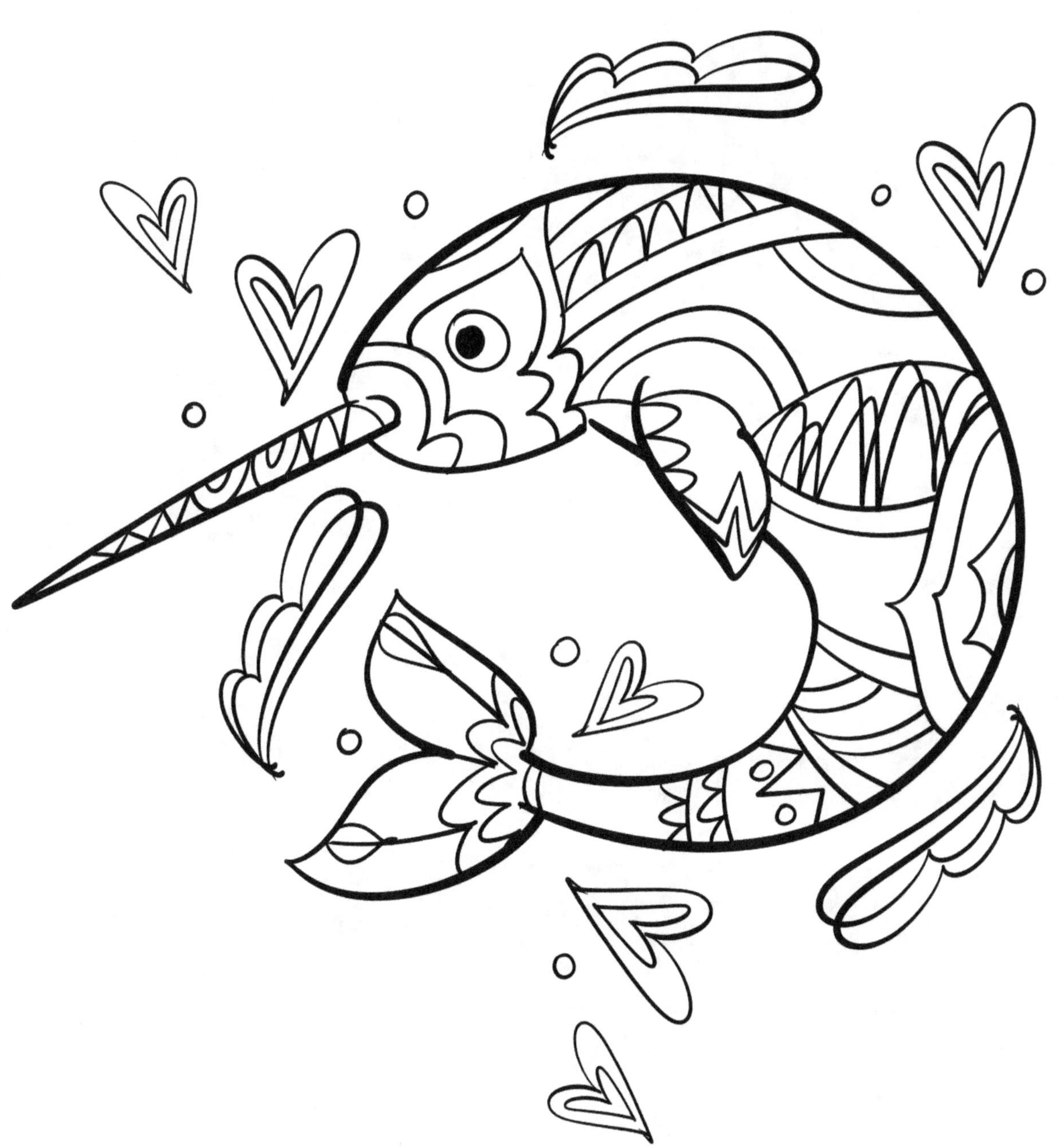

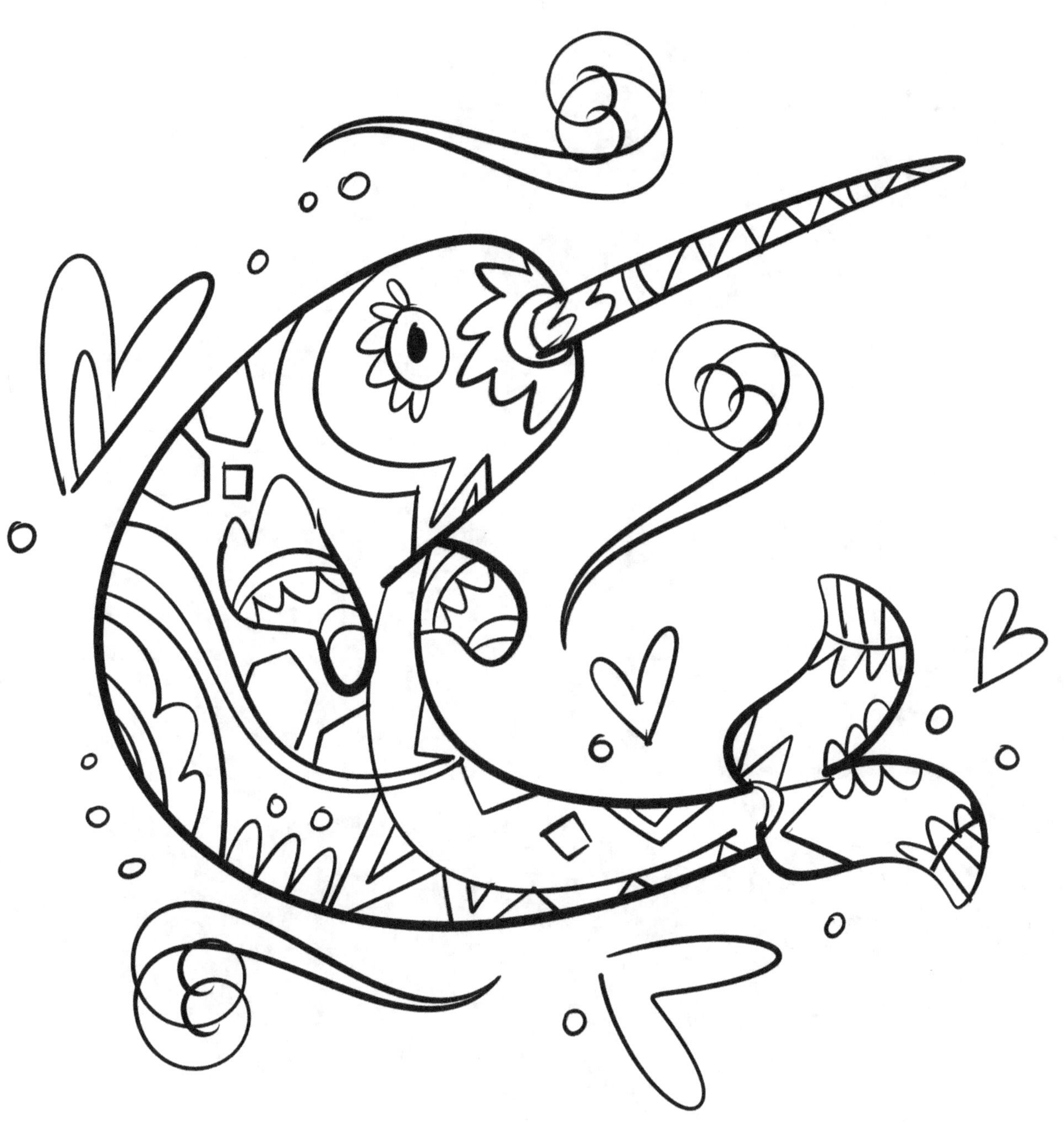

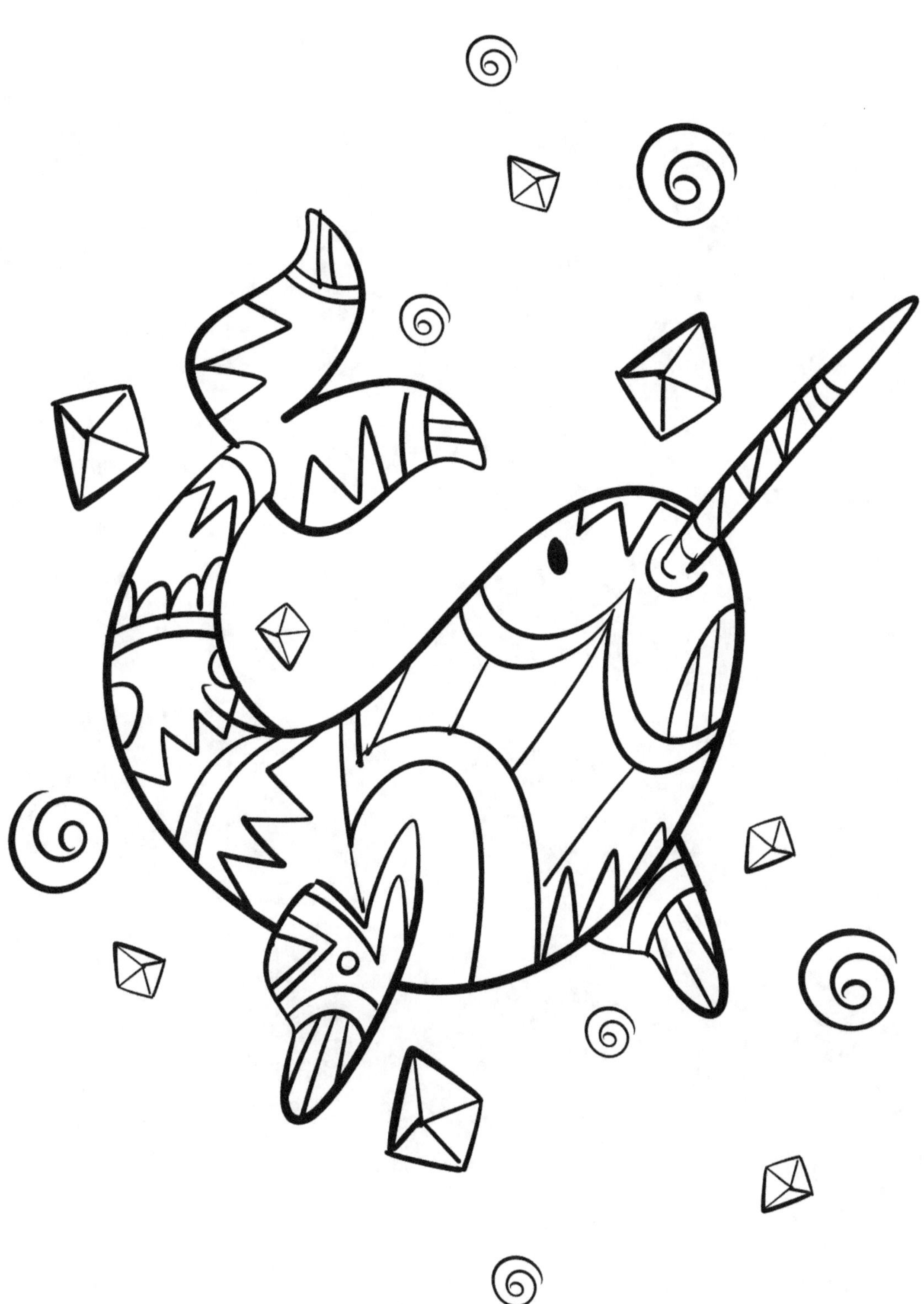

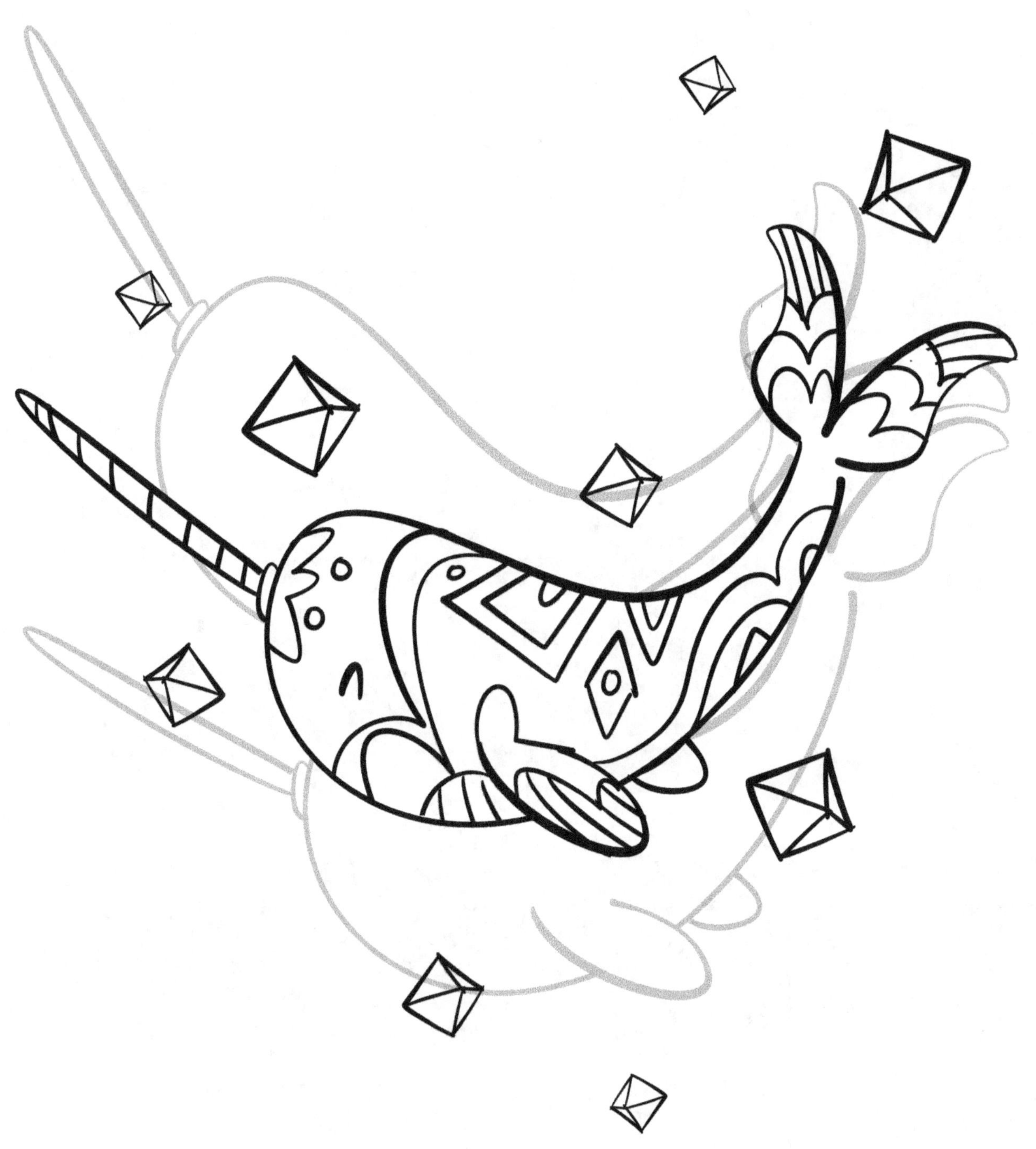

www.ingramcontent.com/pod-product-compliance
Lightning Source LLC
Chambersburg PA
CBHW081501250726
48662CB00009B/3183